A Crabtree Branches Book

I0799385

Today's Stars

JOHN CENA

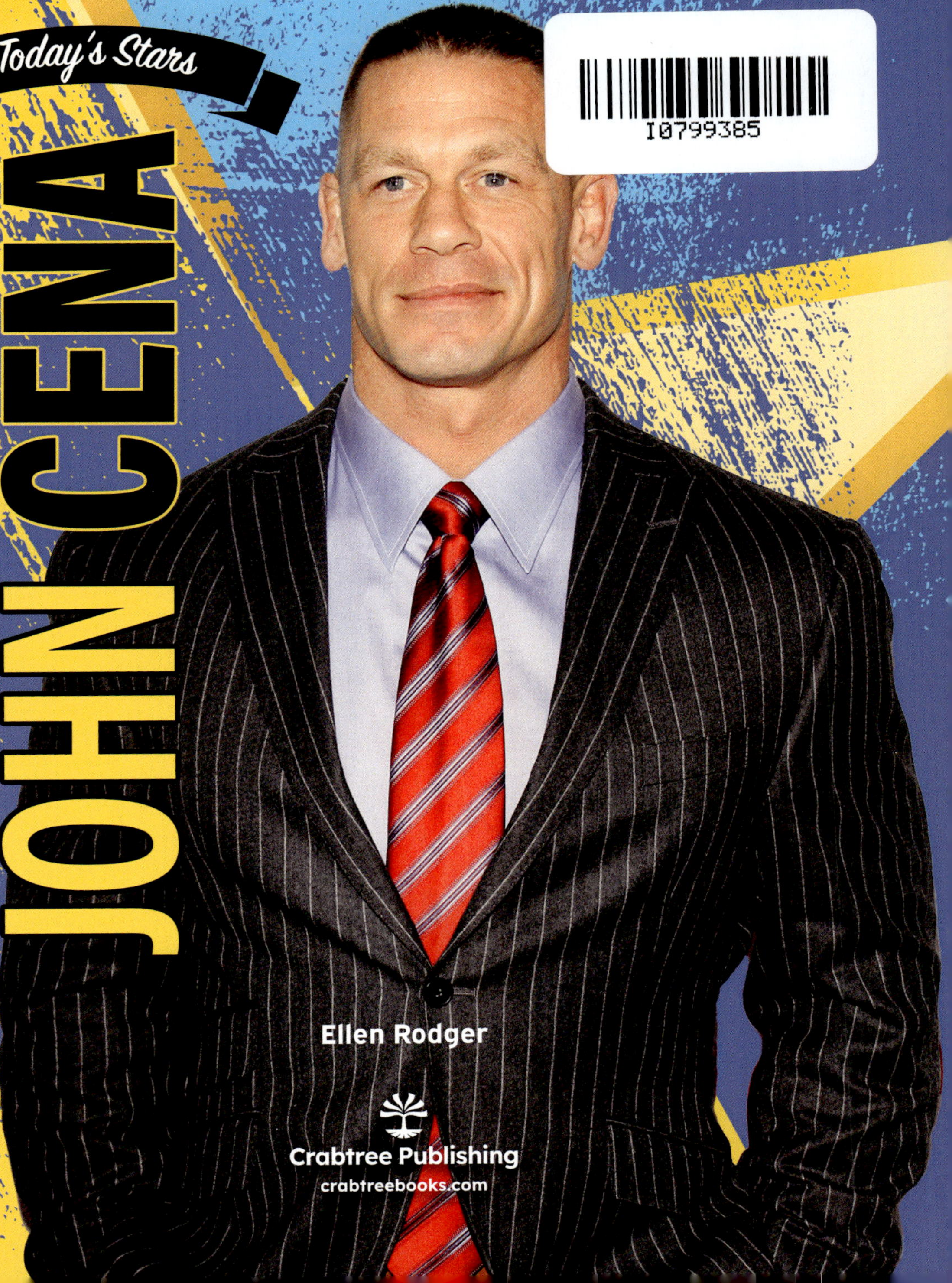

Ellen Rodger

Crabtree Publishing
crabtreebooks.com

School-to-Home Support for Caregivers and Teachers

This high-interest book is designed to motivate striving students with engaging topics while building fluency, vocabulary, and an interest in reading. Here are a few questions and activities to help the reader build upon his or her comprehension skills.

Before Reading:

- *What do I think this book is about?*
- *What do I know about this topic?*
- *What do I want to learn about this topic?*
- *Why am I reading this book?*

During Reading:

- *I wonder why...*
- *I'm curious to know...*
- *How is this like something I already know?*
- *What have I learned so far?*

After Reading:

- *What was the author trying to teach me?*
- *What are some details?*
- *How did the photographs and captions help me understand more?*
- *Read the book again and look for the vocabulary words.*
- *What questions do I still have?*

Extension Activities:

- *What was your favorite part of the book? Write a paragraph on it.*
- *Draw a picture of your favorite thing you learned from the book.*

TABLE OF CONTENTS

BIG GUY, BIG HEART

John Cena is a big guy with a big heart. He is a body builder, professional wrestler, and an actor. John's massive muscles make him seem **menacing**. But he's really very kind and funny. John is known for his "never give up" attitude and his **charitable** works.

John Cena is considered one of the world's greatest professional wrestlers.

John encourages people to learn from their mistakes and be gentle with others who are also learning. He does this through his actions as well as his words. John takes on **characters** in his acting career who are not quite perfect, but always trying.

Fun Facts

As a child, John and his brothers played pretend wrestling. They even made their own championship belts out of cardboard!

DETERMINED ATHLETE

John Felix Anthony Cena was born on April 23, 1977, in West Newbury, Massachusetts. His parents, John and Carol, raised him and his four brothers to have an interest in sports. John's father was a former wrestling **ring announcer**.

As a child, John was bullied. When he was 12, he asked his parents to buy him a weight-lifting bench. This kick-started his interest in body building and professional wrestling.

With a dad who was a wrestling announcer, it may have seemed natural that John would develop an interest in the sport. John was serious about building his body and his personality.

Before becoming a wrestler, John pursued a career in body building.

Fun Facts

John has a college degree in exercise **physiology**. He also played football at Springfield College in Massachusetts. He was team captain!

RISING WRESTLER

All young wrestling fans have an idol. John's was Hulk Hogan. He was inspired by his size, skills, and **charisma**.

John has worked with many of his heroes, including Hulk Hogan, during his long wrestling career.

John got his first break in professional wrestling in 1998 with Ultimate Pro Wrestling (UPW). His character was known as The Prototype. At first, he wrestled in small clubs and arenas, learning new skills along the way.

*As The Prototype, John's character was half-man, half-robot, with **mannerisms** like a powerful machine.*

John earned a Heavyweight Championship in the UPW before signing a **contract** in 2001 to join the World Wrestling Federation (WWF). There, he took on a number of different **personas**, ring names, and nicknames. Over time, his persona changed from a bad guy to a good guy.

The World Wrestling Federation changed its name to World Wrestling Entertainment (WWE) in 2002.

Fun Facts

Wrestling is famous for its nicknames. John has been known as The Champ, The Doctor of Thuganomics, Big Match John, Mr. Money in the Bank, The Face that Runs the Place, and several more.

John has won 21 wrestling championships in his long career. He is a fan favorite, known for his strength and skills as well as his desire to inspire others. WWE has called him the greatest wrestler of all time!

John has won five United States Championships, the most in WWE.

ACTING THE PART

While still wrestling, John began a second career in film and television acting. He has also been a voice actor in cartoons and video games. John's friendly and funny personality led to work hosting reality shows, awards ceremonies, and even game shows!

In the 2017 animated movie Ferdinand, *John voiced the character of a bull who would rather smell flowers than fight.*

John is a four-time Tag Team Champion.

In 2022, John added superhero to his list of talents. He played the part of comic book character Peacemaker both on film and in the television series. The role allowed him to show off more of his comedic skills as a sometimes-bumbling **antihero**.

John has said that Peacemaker is his favorite acting role.

Fun Facts

The Marine was John's first film. He played a marine whose wife was kidnapped by diamond thieves. The film was produced by WWE and released in 2006. More acting roles followed.

THE GOOD GUY

In many of John's films, he plays the good guy, or the funny guy. Even when playing a **villain**, his humor makes him likable.

John was the voice for the mutant rhinoceros named Rocksteady in the animated movie Teenage Mutant Ninja Turtles: Mutant Mayhem.

In between acting, voice acting, and hosting shows, John continued to wrestle. He returned to wrestling full time in 2024. He has announced that he plans to **retire** from the wrestling ring at the end of 2025.

John has been wrestling in WWE events for more than 20 years.

Throughout his wrestling career, John's athletic skills and ability to charm an audience earned him many fans. At WrestleMania XXVIII, he **headlined** a match with The Rock that earned $8.9 million. This was the highest earnings for a live WWE wrestling match.

John considers The Rock to be one of his favorite wrestling opponents.

Fellow wrestlers have praised John as a hard worker. He's a 10-time Slammy Award winner. A Slammy is a WWE award with a statue similar to a Grammy. John has won for Superstar of the Year, Match of the Year, Game Changer of the Year, and more.

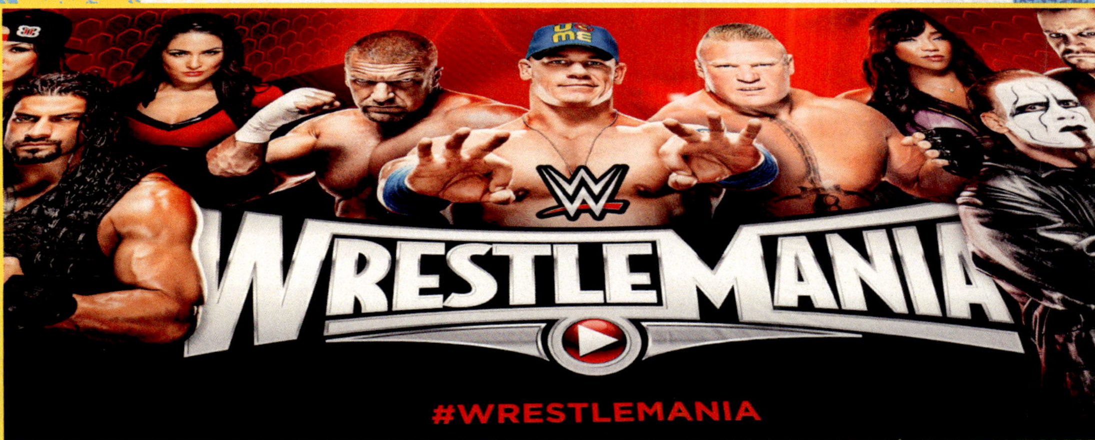

ALL THE LOVE

People love John Cena because he is entertaining. As one of the most popular wrestling stars in the world, he has made a lot of money. He's also given money and time to charities.

John has supported causes such as WWE's "Be a Star" anti-bullying campaign.

Fun Facts

Young people especially like John. But he has tons of fans of all ages. He has said he thinks this is because he is honest and true to himself and people can recognize that.

John holds several records, including 21 total championships and 13 WWE championships. He has also competed in about 1,800 WWE matches—making him third in appearances.

One of John's greatest records is the 650 wishes he granted through the Make-A-Wish Foundation. That's more than anyone else in the world! The charity grants wishes, including celebrity appearance wishes, to children who are seriously ill.

John has said meeting children through Make-A-Wish is "the coolest thing."

GLOSSARY

antihero (AN-tee-heer-oh): A main character of a story, but one that doesn't act like a typical hero

character (KAR-ik-ter): A person represented in a story or play

charisma (kuh-RIZ-muh): A charm or appeal that attracts the attention and admiration of others

charitable (CHAR-i-tuh-buhl): Generous or kind in donations or gifts to others

contract (KON-trakt): A legal agreement between two or more people

headline (HED-lahyn): To lead an event, or have top billing

mannerisms (MAN-uh-riz-uhms): A person's way of moving or talking

menacing (MEN-i-sing): Something that is threatening in actions, attitudes, or ideas

persona (per-SOH-nuh): A character played by a person

physiology (fiz-ee-OL-uh-jee): The science that deals with the functions of living things and their body parts

retire (ri-TAHYUHR): To stop a job or career on a permanent basis

ring announcer (ring uh-NOUN-ser): A person at a wrestling or boxing event who introduces the competitors to the audience

villain (VIL-uhn): A person or character considered to be bad

INDEX

WEBSITES TO VISIT

https://www.wwe.com/superstars/john-cena

https://www.britannica.com/biography/John-Cena

https://kids.kiddle.co/John_Cena

ABOUT THE AUTHOR

Ellen Rodger won a bank-sponsored short story contest at age nine. It was the last thing her bank ever gave her for free, but it kicked-started a career in newspaper, magazine, and book publishing. Ellen has written hundreds of books for curious young people, on topics as varied as the history of the potato, urban wildlife, refugees, the Great Lakes, and explorers.

Crabtree Publishing

crabtreebooks.com 800-387-7650

Copyright © 2026 Crabtree Publishing
All rights reserved. No part of this publication may be reproduced, stored in a retrieval system or be transmitted in any form or by any means, electronic, mechanical, photocopying, recording, or otherwise, without the prior written permission of Crabtree Publishing.

Written by: Ellen Rodger
Designed by: Kathy Walsh
Series Development: James Earley
Editor: Melissa Boyce
Educational Consultant: Marie Lemke M.Ed.
Production manager: Candice Campbell

Hardcover: 978-1-0398-8031-3
Paperback: 978-1-0398-8391-8
Ebook (pdf): 978-1-0398-8151-8
Epub: 978-1-0398-8271-3

Printed in the U.S.A./CP2025

Published in Canada
Crabtree Publishing
616 Welland Ave.
St. Catharines, Ontario
L2M 5V6

Published in the United States
Crabtree Publishing
347 Fifth Ave
Suite 1402-145
New York, NY 10016

Library and Archives Canada Cataloguing in Publication
Available at Library and Archives Canada

Library of Congress Cataloging-in-Publication Data
Available at the Library of Congress

Photographs
Alamy: ZUMA Press p 5, ALLSTAR PICTURE LIBRARY p 12, dpa picture alliance p 15, ZUMAp 17, WENN p 29,
Newscom: Sashenka Gutierrezp 28
Shutterstock: Kathy Hutchins, cover, title page, p 4, p 18-19, p 26; Ga Fullner, TOC; Fred Duval, p 6; Everett Collection, p 8; quiggyt4, p 14; Tinseltown, p 20; chingyunsong, p 22; Sam Aronov, 24, p 25 (bottom); Eric Broder Van Dyke, p 25 (top)
Wikimedia: Creative Commons, p 5 (bottom), p 13, p 16, p 19, p 23, p 27; S. Department of Defense, p 21
All other images by Shutterstock